Meet the family
my Brother

by Mary Auld

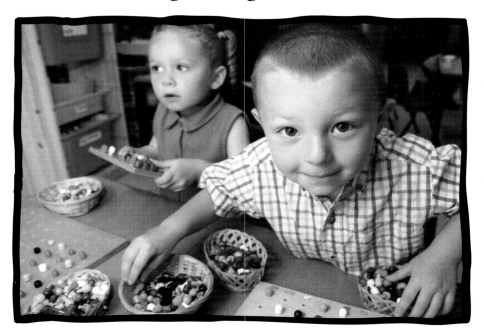

W
FRANKLIN WATTS
Schools Library and Information Services

This is Emma and her brother James with their mum and dad. James is five years younger than his sister Emma.

Nasser's brother is just
a baby. Nasser sometimes
holds him – very carefully.

Heather's brother is her twin. They were born 15 minutes apart.

Claire's older brother David has a different dad.
He is her half-brother.

Steve and Michael are step-brothers. Steve's mum is married to Michael's dad now – but they had Steve and Michael with other people before they met.

Zoe's brother goes
to nursery school.

Andy's brother
has a Saturday job.

Li's brother has
a computer.
He lets Li use it.

Ed likes to do acrobatics
with his brother.

Sometimes Rachel
and her brother fight.

Louise has bike races
with her two brothers.

Molly and her brothers make camps in their back garden.

This is Scot with his mum
and his mum's brother –
Scot's Uncle Carl.

Do you have a brother?
What's he like?

Family words

Here are some words people use when talking about their brother or family.

Names for children:
Brother, Sister; Son, Daughter.

Names for parents:
Father, Daddy, Dad, Pa;
Mother, Mummy, Mum, Ma.

Names of other relatives:
Grandchildren; Grandparents;
Grandmother, Granny, Grandma;
Grandfather, Grandad, Grandpa;
Uncle; Aunt, Auntie; Nephew, Niece.

If we put the word 'Step' in front of a relative's name, it means that we are related to them by marriage but not by birth.

If we put the word 'Half' in front of our brother or sister, it means that one of our parents is the same and the other is different.

A family tree

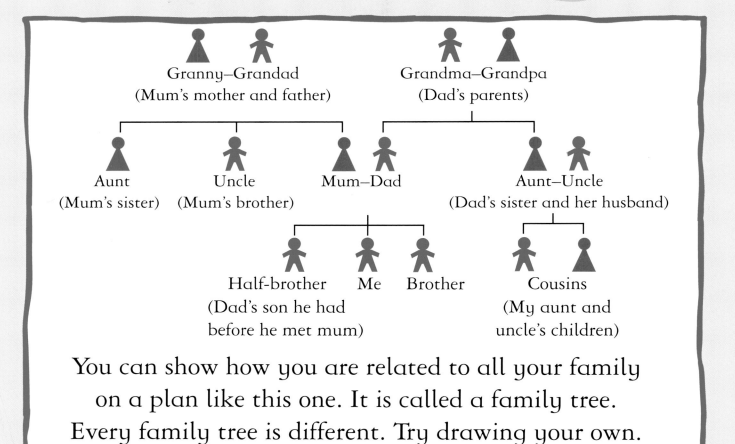

Granny–Grandad
(Mum's mother and father)

Grandma–Grandpa
(Dad's parents)

Aunt
(Mum's sister)

Uncle
(Mum's brother)

Mum–Dad

Aunt–Uncle
(Dad's sister and her husband)

Half-brother
(Dad's son he had
before he met mum)

Me   Brother

Cousins
(My aunt and
uncle's children)

You can show how you are related to all your family
on a plan like this one. It is called a family tree.
Every family tree is different. Try drawing your own.

Published in 2008 by Franklin Watts,
338 Euston Road, London NW1 3BH

Franklin Watts Australia
Level 17/207 Kent Street, Sydney NSW 2000

Copyright © Franklin Watts 2003

Series editor: Rachel Cooke
Art director: Jonathan Hair
Design: Andrew Crowson

A CIP catalogue record for this book
is available from the British Library.
ISBN 978 0 7496 8107 4

Printed in Hong Kong/China

Acknowledgements:
Bruce Berman/Corbis: front cover centre below.
www.johnbirdsall.co.uk: front cover main, 1, 5, 12,
18, 22. Craig Hammell/ Corbis: 9. Judy
Harrison/Format: 17. Carlos Goldin/Corbis: front
cover centre above. Sally Greenhill, Sally & Richard
Greenhill: 16, 19. Ronnie Kauffman/Corbis: 20.
Peter Olive/ Photofusion: 13. Gary
Parker/Photofusion: 6. Jose Luis Pelaez/Corbis: front
cover centre top, 14. George Shelley/Corbis: front
cover bottom. Ariel Skelley/Corbis: front cover
centre. Bob Watkins/Photofusion: 11. Lisa Woollett

Whilst every attempt has been made to clear
copyright should there be any inadvertent omission
please apply in the first instance to the publisher
regarding rectification.

Franklin Watts is a division of Hachette Children's
Books, an Hachette Livre UK company.
www.hachettelivre.co.uk

Please note that some of the pictures in this book
have been posed by models.